# Zion's Heart
## by
## Anthony L Wallace

This book is a work of fiction.
Published in 2018

Peoria, AZ

Other books by Anthony L Wallace

The Escort
The Color of Love
Corner Boy
Ellen
Bad Company

# One

There's nothing like summer in New York City. The streets are buzzing with activity, the sound, sights and smell of the Big Apple is something everyone should have the pleasure of experiencing. And every Sunday at Rucker Park the ball players come out to show their skills. Everyone from high school all Americans to NCAA players and some past and present Professionals come out to run the courts at the world famous park. But today, Zion and his boys are untouchable, three straight wins.

"I'm out. I have to get back, dinner with the family."

"You sure you can't run one more?"

"I'm sure. Look cuz, you got a million guys out here ready to ball. Pick one."

Derek, Zion's first cousin and best friend lives in Harlem with his mom. Zion and him grew up together. Their fathers are brothers, but took different routes in life. Zion's dad went to college, worked hard, now he's one of the wealthiest investors in the state. Derek's father went the street route, which headed straight to incarceration.

"Just one more."

"I can't you know my pop. So I'm out. Plus we can murder these fools next Sunday."

"Damn Derek, your boy talks a lot of shit."

"The name is Zion. Don't act like you're blind."

Journey Renee Maddox, Harlem hustler, runs the streets with the shady types. Her sandy blonde dreads pulled back into a ponytail. Her crew eyes Zion with bad intentions.

"Damn son, you feeling yourself way too hard."

"Not at all."

"You have a safe trip back uptown. It'll be dark soon, it's not safe around here at night." Her crew laughs. Zion smiles. It's funny how he's too black in his zip code, but not black enough down here. It's something that he's been dealing with his whole life. But it still bothers him at times.

"That's a new one."

Maybe she went too far. Her intent wasn't to hurt him. She just wanted to say something to him.

"So where are you from? The only place I ever see you is here. Harlem is not that big."

"I would love to stay and chat. But I have to get back uptown." Zion takes a seat on the pavement next to his bike. He removes his Ray Allen Jordan 13s. He stuffs everything into a Louis Vuitton backpack. He pops in his airpods, slides his feet into his riding shoes.

"Nice bike. What is it?" Asked a random person.

"Thanks. Whyte Glencoe."

Zion waved to his cousin before peddling off. It's about an hour commute to his home on the Upper East Side of Manhattan. At this time of day the traffic would be heavy.

"Hey Derek. Who's that kid?" Journey asked.

"My family."

"Where he from?"
Derek laughs. "Uptown."

James stands at the edge of the patio looking out over the city. The view is breath taking. No where in his widest dreams did he image that he would be living in a nine million dollar home, or sharing it with such an amazing woman, not to mention a wonderful family. He felt truly blessed. Only if his parents were here to enjoy this moment, they would be so proud.

"Hey pop. What you doing out here?"
"Living my best life." He answered.
"We are."
"So how was the game?"
"I left with no L's."
"How's Derek?"
"Good. He's going to see Uncle Kenny this week. I might go with him."

James and his brother haven't seen eye to eye in many years. James blames his brother for their mother's passing. He believes she died from a broken heart when Kenny went to prison. Kenny doesn't seem to care.

"Mom said she's ready to go."

"Zoe, come here, come and give your dad some love."

"Dad you're wasting time. We're going to be late. And you know how much mom hates to be late."

"Tardiness' shows disrespect." Beverly strolls in. If this were a catwalk she would give Naomi Campbell a run for her money. Her little black dress shows off her lean tone body. She kissed James on the lips.

"It's time."


"I love this place."

"So do I mom."

Zion hated going to fancy eateries. It wasn't the food. The food was delicious; the dressing up is what he loathed. If he could wear short pants everyday that would be enough for him, Florida or Arizona was calling him. Just somewhere warm all year long.

"What are your plans this summer?"

Here it comes. Just didn't think it would be this soon. But he had to face the question head on.

"I'm not sure."

"You have options." Beverly said.

Zoe was glad that she was still in high school. Plus she's training all summer on her tennis game.

"Zion, you could go work for your father, or even better yet, you could always come and work for me. Law is in your blood." Beverly did five years for the DA before embracing the dark side.

"No thanks."

The table laughed hard and loud. Others took notice. He didn't mean to spill it out so quickly. But there it was. The truth.

"Well. I guess I know where I stand."

"It's not how it sounds mom."

Right on time, desert, you can't speak with sweets in your mouth.

"Is it okay if I stay with Derek tomorrow night?"

"On a week night?"

"Bel, it's summer. And he's twenty."

"You may." She gave in.

"Man do you ever take the train?" Derek asked.

"Why should I when I have this?"

Zion leaned his bike against the building. He locked the wheels, everything in this area seems to grow legs and walk away. Derek opened a bottle of Poweraide.

"You?"

"No thanks, way too much sugar."

"You ready for this party? It's in a bad part of the city."

"You act like I'm new to this." Zion takes the bottle. Derek knew his cousin was thirsty. He was covered in sweat. Derek opened another bottle.

"You need a shower cus."

"Your mom cool with me staying?"

"Grab your wheels."

Journey entered the room, everyone got quite. It was time to work. She turned off the big screen Samsung. She took the seat next to the television.

"Once you're out, hit Manny for a re-up. I'm going to be with Shake over at the spot. And Please make sure your burner is on."

The street's all she knows. She's been down since day one. Her older brother Frankie started the business a few years ago before getting sent up state. He still calls the shots from inside. Journey's his number two, but Shake is his main man. They go way back. They're like brothers.

Shake rolls a blunt as the rest of the crew prepares to move out. He fires it up. Journey's not a smoker, or drinker. She nods her head. He knows the rules.

"I'm opening a window now."

"Good. You shouldn't be smoking in here anyway."

"I'm sorry, but I got a habit."

"Do you?"

He takes a long drag. He looks over Journey as she makes a plate. "You want some tacos?"

"You know I want some tacos."

"Then you better get in here and make yourself a plate."

Shake puts out the blunt before entering the small kitchen. He pressed his body against Journey's trapping her between himself and the warm stove. He wants her, he always has.

"What are you doing? Back up."

"Don't play so hard to get."

"I'm not playing. Back up Shake."

He moves toward the table. He slowly picks up a paper plate. He's at a lost for words. His ego took a small shot. But he couldn't let that get in the way of business.

"You need to get at Frankie. We're running on scraps out here. It's time to meet with the connect."

"I'm going out there next week."

Next week, they're down to the bare bones now. They won't last to next week. If they wait that long someone else will move in on their turf. And the last thing they need right now is a war.

"You need to speak with him like yesterday. I don't know why he just don't let us meet the plug."

Journey moved back to the living room. She looked around the room. There had to be more. This can't be all that there is. If this is it, she demands a refund. She finished her meal.

"I'm out. Tell your people thanks for the food. I'm going to go and get ready. I'll met you there."

"About ten."

"Ten it is."

She enters the tiny residence trying her best not to make too much noise. Her aunt Kelly and her two boys were on the sofa watching Netflix. They nodded as she passed by. One would think they would be living the good life, with all the junk they sell. Where does all that money go? She's living no better than what she was before she got in the game. She climbed into the shower.

"Don't use all the hot water. I have to work tonight."

"So do I. The boys have to stay with mom. I got business…"

"…Your mom is too tired. You have to stay."

"I'll stay. But you'll be the one to tell Frankie why I didn't make rounds tonight."

"I'll figure it out." Aunt Kelly stated.

Derek presses the button that makes the window go down. The warm night air fills the cabin. Hip-hop music plays on the deck, they nod to the tunes.

"You know we're headed to the Bronx?"

"I do."

Derek sticks his arm out the window. He makes a waving motion with his hand. Zion leans his seat back. He's not much of a party guy. But it's been a while since he has let his hair down.

"You know we're going to the Bronx?" Palmer didn't give much thought to the question. He was just happy to be out with his boy Zion.

"That's why we have insurance."

"You know we're going to stand out like a sore thumb." Derek screams from the back seat. He continues to wave his hand out the window.

"Like the pimps we are."

"Palmer, there's nothing about you that says pimp. I'm sorry, but it's true."

The car comes to a stop. Palmer puts the car in park. He turns down the radio, and then leans his seat back.

"See that's were you're wrong. This eighty thousand dollar Benz, this ten thousand dollar Rolex and lets not forget, my last name screams pimp, in a major fucking way." Zion and Derek had to agree. Palmer was right. Everything about Palmer was pimp, but not in the way that Palmer saw it.

"Lets go in here and pimp this bitch out."

Derek said. "Please don't talk like that once we get inside." Palmer smiled. He climbs out of the car.

"Don't hate. You know what it is Derek."

The party was in a beat up building in the Gun Hill section of the city. People stood out front smoking and drinking, music blurred from a few different apartments. Palmer by no means was a chicken, but this might have been a bad idea. The elevator smelled of urine and weed.

"We have to get off at the next floor. I don't want to be smelling like piss while I'm spiting game." Derek smiled. Palmer's a wild boy. They exited the elevator. The floor was packed with people, chatting, smoking, drinking and some even dancing. The guys were way over dressed. Zion followed behind Derek. He knew these people. But the goons at the door were high, and looking for trouble.

"Who are you niggas?" Derek tried to smooth things over. But the doormen had other plans. "You niggas are in the wrong spot. Shit about to get ugly real quick." Just then Journey and her people came strolling up the crowed hallway. This wasn't Harlem, but they knew her and more importantly, who her people were. Drake's song After Dark was coming from the apartment. Journey grabbed Zion's hand.

"They're with me." She led him through the sea of people to a tight area where everyone was dancing. He couldn't take his eyes off of her. She pulled him close. His knees went limp. She wrapped her arms around his neck. She smelled wonderful. He wanted to kiss her. They grooved to the beat, their bodies moved as one.

"Damn Dee, Zion is in there." Derek was concerned. Journey was trouble. Derek knew how she got down, and how her people got down. People who made their way to her bad side seem to fall off the face of the earth to never be seen again.

Palmer said. "I'm going to mingle, text me if you need anything." Derek spotted a group of guys from Harlem. He may his way over. Zion's a big boy, he couldn't keep an eye on him all night.

"What's up?"

Mike, a short stocky guy with cornrows and a soft spot for cats smokes a blunt. The group is made up of ex-ballers. "I know you don't what to hit this Derek?" Mike asked.

"I'm good. I'm working out. I'm trying to make the AAU summer team."

Mike wished that he had stayed the course. Zion held her so tight. He didn't want to let go, and she didn't want him to. But the song was coming to an end. And she had business to take care of. Shake strolled in with six hardcore thugs. They were muscle, to make sure that the sellers got paid, and that no one tried to jack them at the end of the night.

Derek could feel the shift and knew it was time to leave. Parties in the Bronx seem to always end with someone shot or worst. He made his way over to Palmer. Palmer was dancing with a girl who could pass for a younger Kelly Rowland.

Derek spotted Zion, but it was too crowed. It was impossible to get to him. Journey made eye contact with Zion. She smiled. He smiled back.

He wanted to ask for her phone number. Before he could open his mouth. She placed her finger on his lips.

"We'll see each other again if it's meant to be." And with that she turned and walked away. He stood in the middle of the dance floor wondering what the hell just happened. He wanted to follow her. He needed to see her again. But she was gone. Just then Derek pulled his arm.

"I think some shit's about to pop off." Zion and Derek found Palmer in the hallway trading spit with a young lady. They gather their friend. The walk back to the car was filled with laughs.

"Man how are you kissing a chick you just met?"

Palmer's stroll took on a whole new attitude. He unlocked the car. He slowly climbed in. He closed the door, and then turned on the ride. He slightly turned so he could see Derek.

"I told you that I was a pimp." The car filled with laughter. Palmer put the car in drive. They drove away feeling pretty good on how the night was going.

Journey and her crew gathered around a booth close to the door. They wanted to see everyone that came in, and if need be, they were close to the only exit.

"It was lit in there tonight. I moved everything."

Journey placed a backpack on the table. All of the runners placed their earnings in the bag. It was a good night, the bag filled up quick. Shake closed the bag and placed it next to him. The small café was getting crowded fast. Journey waved over the waitress. She was short and round; her hair was pulled back into a short ponytail. Journey let her crew order first, and then she ordered a chicken salad. Suddenly the door swung open and a cocky rich white boy entered, followed by his two friends. Journey noticed Zion as he slid into his booth.

"I tell you man. She's checking for you something serious." Zion's confused.

"What are you talking about?"

Palmer waved over the same waitress before saying. "The girl you were dancing with at the party. She's eye balling you right now."

Palmer motions toward the door. Zion slowly turns to get a look. Journey notices his effort to get a glance. She looks away before he sees her looking at him. Zion's heart starts to beat faster. He's truly taken by her.

"I'm going over."

"Do your thing son." Palmer doesn't want the night to end. Derek on the other hand, just wants to eat and head home.

"I'll be back." Zion approaches the table. He's met with mean stares. Journey gives him the not now look. He ignores it.

"Hey." He addresses the group. No one response. He feels the pressure. But he can't tuck and run now. "May I speak with you?" Journey smiles. Shake can't believe that this bitch ass nigga is even still standing there.

"We're in the middle of something right now. So step the fuck off." Shake said with hate in his voice.

"I'm sorry. But I'm not talking to you. I'm speaking to the young lady."

The crew was on edge now. They wanted to stomp Zion out. They're just waiting for the word. Shake's finger was ready to pull the trigger. He held the gun tight under the table. He wanted to put two in him so bad. Journey was impressed, not by his fearlessness to stand up to Shake. But how he never took his eyes off of her.

She spoke up before things got out of hand. "Thank you for coming over. And thank you for the dance. You have a good night."

"Yeah nigga, you have a good night."

Zion takes the walk of shame back to his table. Derek and Palmer are too busy eating to notice what accorded. Zion takes a seat. He looks over his food. The plate is still warm.

"What happened?" Derek asked.

"I can tell you what happened. My man got the number and in a few days he'll get the booty." Palmer said. Zion couldn't disappoint. He didn't say anything. The guys ended the night sitting in the hallway outside of Derek's apartment.

"You can stay if you want." Derek told Palmer.

"I'm good. I think I'm stop by this little shorty's place. You know how I do."

"I hate to be the one to stop the party. But I'm heading to bed."

"I forgot, Zion has to be in bed at a certain time." Palmer said as he tried to stand up. Derek grabbed him before he fell to the floor. Zion shook his head.

"Palmer, I think you should call it a night. Stay here with Derek and I." Palmer wasn't even trying to hear that. He had pussy lined up.

"I'm heading in. I'm beat. " The guys followed him inside.

Journey laid on the bed; she watched a lone roach make its way up the wall. She pulled out her cell. She had no messages or missed calls. She couldn't sleep. All she could think about was the ride to go see her brother Frankie upstate. It's a long ride. She hates the ride. But someone has to make it, and that someone just happens to be her.

She climbed out of bed. Maybe a shower would help her relax. Just then her cell went off. She had a message. She could tell by the tone that it was from Shake. She could check it later. In no time the bathroom was filled with steam.

Zion was up early. He tried his best not to wake Derek. No such luck. "You out?" Zion wanted to stay, but he had to get his ten miles in. He slipped into his riding shoes. "I hate to break out like this. But I have to get my workout in." Zion picked up his bike and headed for the door.

As he rode the city the morning air was warm and thick. He picked up the pace. He was really going for it. Just as he turned the corner a familiar face caught his attention. He slammed on the brakes. The tires screamed as they latched onto the pavement. He made a quick uturn. He peddled hard and fast to catch up. His eyes didn't deceive him. It was she.

"Good morning." He said.

She wasn't paying attention. He surprised her. She smiled. He rode along aside her as she walked. He was out of breath.

"I didn't think I would see you again so soon."

"So, you just knew you would see me again?"

He laughed. "You will be at the Rucker Sunday?"

He was right. She would be there with her crew. The Rucker was a money spot. There's a lot smokers that visit the park.

"What are you doing out so early?"

"If you most know. I'm on my way to visit someone."

He didn't want to seem pushy. But he had to know. "I hope it's not a boyfriend visit."

She thought he was a little noisy. But she answered anyway. "It's a family visit."

"May I walk with you?" He asked.

A gentleman, she wasn't use to that. There's not too many of those living in the five boroughs.

She would love his company, just not today. She had a lot on her mind. She smiled. "No worries. Maybe next time." He stated. He reached into his bag and pulled out a business card.

"My contact information. Next time you take a stroll and want some company. I'm only a phone call away."

"Thank you."

"You have a nice visit."

They parted ways. He rode off feeling good about the encounter. She liked him. But she has no time for boys. She had a business to run, and a family to look after. She made it to the bus station with time to spare.

Zion and Palmer walked down to coffee shop. Zion leaned back in his chair. Palmer was sipping on ice mocha. He only likes coming to this shop so he can flirt with the waitress.

"Shit, man I thought that sexy waitress would be working today."

"You only came over to see some girl?"

Palmer couldn't lie. But he did. Zion wasn't pressed about the situation. He was just happy to see his boy.

"I ran into girl from the party this morning."

"What girl?"

Zion said. "The girl I was dancing with at the party."

"Oh, you mean Journey?"

"You knew who I was talking about."

Palmer never forgets a name, or face. He's weird like that. He soaks up information like a sponge. He takes a small sip.

"I did. So you get the number?"

Zion was ashamed to admit it. "I didn't. But I did give her my business card."

"Your business card? Really? You have no pimp game." Palmer finished his drink. He pitched into the trash. He was ready to go. Zion wasn't so sure of his choice to give Journey his card. Would she call? Was it a bad look? Did he make a huge mistake? Only time will tell.

"The girl from the hallway. You know the one I was tonguing down? She called me today. But I didn't get her name that night so I didn't know what to call her."

"You put your tongue in her mouth but you didn't get her name."

Palmer didn't have an answer. So he just said. "I would've put something else in her as fine as she was. Hell I didn't need her name."

"I hope your lips fall off. I'm done with you."

"You ready? I'm ready to blow this place."

Zion finished his drink. "Let bounce."

Rucker's packed. Derek and Zion sit on the bench. After winning two games they met their match. More than lightly they won't get to play again, at least not today. Journey and her crew enter the park. She's looking but not looking for Zion. He notices her.

"Man I'm about to be out." Zion said to Derek.

"I know. I hate to lose. It takes for ever to get back up."

Zion gives Derek dap and then heads for his bike. He gives Journey a nod as he passes. She does the same. She stops, turns and follows after him. Shake takes notice.

"Hey." She said.

Zion unlocks his wheels. He takes seat on the ground. He removes his game shoes and puts everything in his backpack.

Journey said. "Hey you."

"Hey to you. Did you have a nice visit?"

" It was okay. Nothing to write home about."

He slides into his riding shoes. She turns, Shake is looking her way. She turns her attention back to Zion. "I'm ready for some company on my next stroll."

Zion smiles. "I would be honored."

"You have to go now? She asked.

"I do. I'm staying with my parents for the summer. My mom has a strict dinner time policy."

"For the summer?"

"Yes, I'm on summer break. I'm in my second year at Harvard."

"Harvard? Well damn."

"And you been treating me like I'm some community college drop out."

" Whatever."

"I'm sorry, but I really do have to go."

"I'll call."

"I'll be waiting."

He saddles his bike. He waves to Derek. He peddles off.

Zion and his father sit at the table playing a game of chess. Zoe was resting in a lawn chair reading the novel The Hate You Give. Mom enters the patio with a glass of wine and a beer in the other hand.

"Here you go babe."

Dad takes the beer. He makes a move. Zion looks defeated. He studies the broad. Mom takes a seat next to her son.

She says. "You're in a bad situation."

"What would you do?" He asked. Dad smiles. He's still got it. Mom tries her best to find a way out.

"Two moves and its checkmate." Dad stated. Zion played his best game and he still on the losing end. He tried to go back and find where he went wrong. What move put him in this dreadful spot? Mom rubbed his shoulder.

"You'll get him one day." She said.

"Today is not that day." Dad said with a big laugh. Just then Zion's phone rings. Saved by the bell, he said to himself. Mom waved Zion over so she could have a go at dad.

"You're no better than your son at this game. You sure you're prepared for this beating?"

"I'm not Zion. Don't forget I taught you this game."

"And the student has become the master." He said with a devilish grin. Mom paid him no attention as she setup her pieces. Zion headed to his room. He didn't realized the number, but he hoped that it was Journey calling.

"Hello."

A sweat voice came through and entered his ear. It was she. His heart started to beat at a racers pace. He fell onto his bed.

"You called."

"I told you that I would."

"Indeed you did. I'm happy to hear from you."

"So now what?" All of this was new to her. Most guys were too afraid to speak to her once they learned who her brother is. But Zion, he wasn't from Harlem. He didn't know her about her family, or her brother.

She took a seat and then leaned against the wall. The apartment was too loud, and too crowded. She needed her own space. She needed room to spread out.

"How was dinner?"

"Great. My mom, she's a great cook."

"Really?"

"Yes. Maybe one day you'll find out for yourself."

"Maybe. So you go to Harvard?"

Zion rolled off the bed. He made his way to his bathroom. He studied himself in the mirror. "I do."

"What are you studying?"

"Pre law."

Some kids raced passed her. They made a bunch noise as they horse played. "Sounds like you have a house full." He said.

"I do, but I'm in the hallway. Just some kids."

"Have you always lived in Harlem?"

"I have. Born and raised. You?"

"Manhattan, Upper East Side." He could hear her laughing on the other side. She tired to cover her phone.

"What's so funny?" He asked.

"I knew it. I knew you were a rich boy."

"My parents have money. But I have none."

"They have money, so you have money."

"Is that how it works?"

"It does."

"I see. My parents may have a different opinion."

"I don't mean to cut you short. But I have to go."

"Would you like to have lunch with me? He asked.

"Okay."

"Is that a yes?"

"Yes, it's a yes."

He couldn't hold back his excitement. He did a little jig in the mirror. "I'll call you soon."

"Okay." She ended the call. She couldn't explain the feeling that she was feeling. It was new, but she liked it.

Zion rejoined his family out on the patio. Mom was helping Zoe play dad in a game of chess that she had no chance of winning.

"Happy that you returned."

"I had a call."

Zoe said. "A girl. He only leaves the room when it's a girl."

"What do you know about it?" Mom asked.

"I don't know anything. I'm too busy with tennis."

Dad and mom laughed. Zoe pitched a pawn at her big brother. They spent the rest of the night chatting.

# Two

Lunchtime in the city is just as bad as rush hour traffic. Zion was lucky enough to find a parking spot just a couple blocks away. He checked his watch. He was twenty minutes early. He slowed his pace. He entered Settepani and then gave his name to the hostess.

"I see I'm not the only one who likes to be early." Journey said with a smile.

She's beautiful, casually dressed, but still beautiful. Zion couldn't hold back his joy. Joy in his face warmed her heart.

"I'm little under dressed." She stated.

"Not at all. I had a presentation today."

They followed the hostess to their table. The natural light shinning in through the big windows gave Journey this amazing glow. Her smile was big and bright.

"So, this presentation, was it for your law career?"

"Not at all. I do MLM on the side. It was for that."

"MLM?"

"Network Marketing. Direct Sales, like Mary Kay, Avon and so on."

"Oh, so you sell Avon?"

He laughed. "No, I'm with the company Lifevantage. We're a health and wellness company."

"I can see that. You look like the kind of guy who's into his body."

"Body and mind."

"That's still to be seen."

They spoke more than they ate. Their body language suggested that they were life long friends. She hasn't laughed this much in a long time. Once they finished their meal they took a stroll through Lower Harlem.

"Why did you pick that place?" She asked.

"You're from Harlem. I wanted you to feel comfortable."

"Thank you."

"I hope I'm not being too forward when I say I would love to see you again."

Journey felt the same way. But she couldn't show it. She wanted to, but something deep down kelp her guards up.

"Okay."

"Is that a yes?"

"Yes, I would like to see you again."

"Let me give you a ride home."

"I'm going to Uber it."

Out of the question. He wanted to spend more time with her. Plus they could chat a little more on the ride. He couldn't let her get away so easily. He took her hand. She followed his lead.

"You don't have to give me a ride. I'm a big girl, and lets not forget. I'm from Harlem."

"My dad would kill me if he knew that I let you take an Uber."

"I don't want your father to kill you."

"Great, neither do I."

"Nice car. A or S?"

"I see you know your Audis. But she's an RS."

He opened the door for her. She slid in. As he made his way around to the driver's side she leaned over to unlock his door. He started the car. Journey leaned her seat back. The AC came rushing out of the vents. It felt good to get out of the summer heat.

"Do you have to be anywhere?" He asked.

She did, but it could wait. "No. What do you have in mind?"

"Lets take a ride."

"Can I drive?" She asked. Zion had only one rule. No one sits behind the wheel of his baby. He's put a lot of long nights and cash into getting her just where he wanted her.

"Drive? She's totally modified. I'm not sure you can handle such a beast."

"Son please, I can drive anything."

"That may be, but…"

She cut him off mid sentence. "…Am I driving or not?" Zion removed his seatbelt. Journey rushed out of the car. Zion took his sweet time exiting.

"Don't worry. I'll be nice.". Zion wasn't so sure about this. But he made a promise to himself to step out of his comfort zone.

"Take it easy. She has a lot of pull."

Journey adjusted her seat, then the mirrors. She leaned her seat back. Zion tightened his seatbelt. Journey turned the key. The engine roared to life.

"Oh, that sounds good." Journey said.

Zion said. "Make sure to look before you pull out." Journey laughed.

"Sit back and relax." She slammed on the gas the tires screams as they pulled out. The Audi had more power than she imaged. She turned on the radio. Zion turned down the music. The light turned green and car shot out like a bat out of hell.

"Slow down. You don't want to get a ticket."

"Will you please relax. I'm not going to hurt your car."

"I know. I just don't want you to get into trouble."

"You're so sweat."

"Where are you headed?"

Journey said with a grin. "Interstate 87. I thought we would cruise up to University Heights."

Zion turned up the radio. He leaned back and relaxed as Journey weaved in and out of traffic. She had skills. He pulled out his Iphone to check his messages.

"Make sure you let them college girls know not to text you anymore."

"You make sure you tell them thugs not to hit you up."

She smiles. She didn't know what to think. She likes him, but they come from two different worlds. Would it work? Could it work? Zion didn't give a seconds thought of the dynamics of what this thing was or wasn't. He was happy in the moment. They chatted the whole ride. And she drove.

She pulled over at W 126$^{th}$ street and Malcolm X Blvd. She had to check in on her runners. She turned the car off. She undid her seatbelt.

"I had a great time today. Thanks for lunch. And thanks for letting me drive your baby."

"Don't tell me that our day is coming to an end."

"I have things I need to do."

"Okay. I'll talk to you later."

"If you're lucky."

They exited the car at the same time. She held the door open for him. He wanted to kiss her. They were close enough to kiss. But he was unsure. So instead he gave her a huge hug. She thought it was cute.

She said. "Call me later."

"Will do."

He climbed in and drove off. She watched as he disappeared into traffic. She slowly made her way to the spot. She knocked on the door, a giant of a man with a deep scare on his face answered. He smiled as held the door for her.

"Hey big man. How you doing?"

"I'm good." He answered.

Before she entered he said. "He's not happy."

She knew he wouldn't be. But that's life. She made her way to the bar. The crew was sitting around the table. Shake was smoking and drinking, he wasn't in a good mood.

"Where the fuck have you been?" He asked as he passed the blunt. She motioned for the guy to move.
She took the seat and the blunt.

"I was busy. I didn't have my burner."

"Really? Is that what you're going to tell Frankie?   She knew that she was going to have to face her brother. She would cross that bridge soon enough. She put it out on the bottom of her shoe before passing it back.

"Don't everyone start talking at once."

"Well…" Mike started to say.

Shake cut him off "…So now you're interested?"

"Nigga get out of your feelings and tell me what the fuck happened. I don't have time for this bitch shit."

Shake knew that he was Frankie's number two. But his baby sister would always be his number one. So no matter how he felt he couldn't put hands on her. She asked again. "What happened?"

"The connect pushed up the deadline."

"By how much?"

"A lot. We don't have it."

She didn't want to hear that. Even though she knew it was true. Not having the money could be bad for everyone involved.

"How short are we?" She asked.

"You don't want to know." Shake said.

"Why would the connect even think we would be able to get that much paper in such a short amount of time?"

"That's a question for big brother." Shake said.

"We might have to out source some of this work. I know you guys don't want to work with these other crews. But this could be a win for all of us."

"How are your going to get them to slang our shit? They all have their own hook ups."

"True, but we got the best shit in town. Plus we might have to give it to them at a discount." She said.

"Fuck that. That takes money out of our pockets. And you know Frankie's not going to go for that." Shake said.

"He has no choice. If we can't pay the connect. We're all dead." Shake knew she was right. But he couldn't take less. He was barely making it now.

"I have to go. I'll talk to Frankie" Journey said as she stood up and prepared to leave.

Zion stood in front of a large flat screen as he did his presentation. He loved making his own way. Network Marketing gave him the opportunity to help others. The room was packed with team members and prospects alike. Zion was a master of words. He made everything sound righteous.

After the event he mingled with friends. He signed up three new distributors and a couple of new customers.

"You're really building this business." Donna said as she looked around the room.

"I'm taking it one day, one person at a time."

"You're doing it."

"Thank you. I don't know where I would be without you mentoring me. You have a lot to do with my success."

"No, I don't. You did all the work." She said as she gave him a big hug.

Then she said. "I have to go. But I'll be in contact tomorrow."

"Goodnight. Thank you for coming out."

Zion packed up his belongings. He said his good byes and then headed for the parking lot. The night air was thick. He decided to stop off for a quick bite at the Shake Shack. He took a seat at a near by table.

"What did you get?"

He turned, and there stood Journey. She smiled. Ever the gentleman he stood to offer her a seat.

"The Chicken Shack. And you? What did you order?"

"Just a plain ole burger." She said.

He couldn't take his eyes off of her. She loved the way he looked at her. She felt like a schoolgirl experiencing her first real crush.

"I'm sorry I haven't returned any of your calls. I've been sort of busy these last few days."

He said. "No problem. I had a busy schedule as well."

"You coming to the park Sunday?"

"Will you be there?" He asked.

"You can't answer a question with a question."

He adored her smile. She seemed to smile whenever she spoke to him. He inched closer to her. She welcomed him. He took her hand in his.

"You still haven't answered the question."

"Yes. I like you. And I want to continue to see you."

She looked away for a second, then she turned back to him. "Still, that's not the question."

"I will be there Sunday. I'll be there schooling those fools like I do every Sunday."

She laughed. And then she said. "I would like to see you again." She wanted to grab those words and put them in here pocket as soon as they left her mouth. The words were true. She did want to see him again. But there was a price to pay. Did she have the funds to make such a payment?

"You ready to blow this joint?"

"I am."

He gathered their trash and pitched in a near by container. They strolled the park. He pulled her close. She didn't resist.

"Maybe we can do dinner Sunday with the folks." He said.

"Are you going to ask for my hand in marriage?"

"Somewhere down the line. Give it some time. Don't rush things." He said.

"You need to stop."

He said. "I'm just saying."

She wrapped her arm around his. She layed her head on his shoulder as they walked, she felt comfortable with him. Just then a group of loud teens bumped into them. One of the boys was rude and looking for trouble.

"Excuse me." Zion said.

"Damn son, watch where the fuck you're walking." The teen said.

Zion tried to defuse the situation. But the boys weren't having any of it. All for one and one for all. That's how they rolled.

"My bad. Forgive." Zion said as he and Journey tired to move on.

"Fuck that my bad shit, nigga." One of the boys recognized Journey, and knew that his friend was making a life-threatening mistake.

He said to his friend. "Chill. Chill man that's Journey."

He went from a 100 to 0 real quick. He said. "I'm sorry. I'm tripping. I've been drinking. I know that's not an excuse to act that way. Like I said. I'm sorry. I didn't mean anything by it."

Before Journey could say anything Zion waved the boys off. As they went on their way Journey asked.

"Why didn't you knock that jerk out?"
"No foul. No harm."

She wasn't use to letting people step to her. She wanted to do something to him, to let him know that she wasn't someone to play with. She wanted to run back and slap the shit out of the guy. It was eating at her.

Zion could feel her tense up. He pulled her close. He whispered in her ear.

"You don't have to be so tough. I got you."

The next few weeks they spent everyday together, going to the park, visiting the museums. They even took a tour to see a few historic landmarks. Journey has lived her whole life in the Big Apple and never thought about visiting Lady Liberty.

"I think it's time to meet the family."

Journey said. "You sure you want to do that?"

"I was thinking the same thing. I'm the cool one in my family. So don't expect too much."

Journey said. "My family's no picnic."

Zion opened the door. Journey slowly stepped out. Her dress was classy, her hair pulled back. Zion took her by the hand.

"Don't worry. They're going to love you."

"This is where you live?"

"Don't let it intimidate you. It's just a house."

Journey swallowed hard. "Yeah, a very big house."

They entered. The beauty of the home took journey; it was big, big and spacious, she didn't want to touch anything. Everything looked expensive. Zoe called out from the kitchen. "We're in here."

Zoe and Bel were finishing up. Journey was unsure of herself. She was fidgeting. Beverly noticed.

"You must be Journey? I'm Beverly, and this is Zion's little sister Zoe."

Zoe said. "Younger sister."

"Where's dad?"

Beverly glanced at her watch. "He should be here shortly. He had some last minute business at the office."

Zoe said. "Would you like to join us?"

"Sure. Why not?" Journey answered.

Zion noticed that Journey still had her shoes on. He waved her over. He kneeled down. Journey's heart was beating twice as fast as normal. It was hard for her to catch her breath.

"What are you doing?" She asked.

He reached and then undid her shoe. She smiled. She couldn't believe what she was thinking. She stepped out of her shoes.

"All things in due time." He said.

"I'm heading back to the kitchen."

James entered the house. He waved as he headed to the bedroom. Beverly chased him down. He never entered the house without greeting his family. Something was wrong. She found him in the bathroom. The door was closed. She knocked.

"What's wrong?" She asked.

He yelled back. "I went to lunch with Jones. I got the bubble guts."

She tried not to laugh. But she couldn't help it.

She laughed hard. "Zion's little friend is here. Don't be too long."

He said. "I'm hit the shower and then I'll be right down."

"Okay. Love you."

"Love you."

James joined everyone out on the patio. Zoe and Beverly hurried to the kitchen to retrieve dinner.

"Dad, this is my friend Journey." James shook her hand. He had a firm grip she thought. But his hands were soft and smooth. He hasn't done any physical labor in years.

"Dinner is served." Beverly said as she laid everything on the table.

"It smells and looks so good Mrs. Matthews."

"Thank you. And thank you for your help."

"I didn't do much." Journey said.

James said. "Lets dig in."

After dinner Zoe went to a friend's house. James, Beverly, Zion and Journey chatted as they relaxed at the table.

"So Journey. How do you and Zion know each other?" Beverly asked.

"We met at Rucker."

"I've been trying to get dad to come out and ball with Derek and I."

James said. "You guys don't want me to come out there and show you young bucks up."

The table had a good laugh. Beverly was still trying to figure Journey out. She could tell that Journey was street smart. But she needed to know more. In her eyes, whomever was lucky enough to land Zion had to be from the right side of the tracks.

"Where did you go to school? Zion went to Regis. I bet you went to Brearley. Zoe's in her second year."

"I went to Frederick Douglas."

James said. "Tough school."

Journey said. "From what I hear it's worst now."

This was strike one in Beverly's eyes. A good education is one main ingredient for a successful future. James poured his wife another glass of wine.

"So what are you doing now? You in school?"

"Mom, what's with all the questions?"

"I'm sorry I don't mean to pry."

James sipped his wine. He could care less about Journey's past. They were young; it wasn't like they were getting married tomorrow. Beverly wanted to know more.

"No, I'm not in school. I work for my brother. We have a little carrier business. We're not making millions or anything. But we're doing good."

"Business owners. We need more of us doing exactly what your brother is doing." James said.

"We're trying." Journey said.

Beverly wasn't impressed. "What's the name of the company?" Journey's quick on her feet, she spitted out.

"Maddox Carriers."

"Maddox? I know that name."

Journey said. "Thank you for inviting me into you home. Dinner was great. I have an early morning."

"It was a pleasure to meet you. We must do this again." James said. Beverly said nothing. She was searching her mental roller decks. Zion could see his mom's wheels turning. But he was use to her not warming up to his dates. She was funny like that, too protective, more like overly protective.

"I won't be out too late." Zion said as he and Journey prepared to leave. Zion picked up her shoes on the way out. She took his hand. They walked to his car.

"I really had a good time. I like your family. Your sister is really cool. Not so sure your mom is feeling me."

"I'm feeling you. I hope that's enough."

It was more than enough. She couldn't hold back her smile. His words touched her in way that couldn't be explained. She pulled him close. Her lips softly pressed against his. He was in heaven. He didn't want to let her go. This is where he wanted to be. She pulled back.

"I have an early morning. So I have to go."

"Not now. Don't go." Zion begged.

"I feel your excitement. But I do have to go."

He opened the door. She slowly climbed in. He wanted to pull her back out and tongue her down. He was over heated. If just one kiss got him to this point he could only image what a make session would do to him.

He walked to her building. The goons where out looking for trouble and a quick buck, it was feeding time at the zoo. Shake leaned against the railing surrounded by his boys.

"What do we have here?"

"I'm good here Zion. I have some things I have to take care of. Thank you for the wonderful evening."

She kissed him on the cheek and then turned her attention to her crew. Shake wanted to put his hands on Zion.

"Boy, you're in the wrong part of town."

Zion took a step toward Shake. His boys cut him off. Shake said. "Naw, let the young lad through."

Zion got face to face with Shake. Journey was shocked but also worried. Shake is quick to pull a weapon.

"I'm guessing by the look of you. You're around 30 or 35. You're out here trying to act hard and impress a bunch of twenty year olds. How sad. Let me put it to you like this. I'm open to dance one on one anytime, anyplace."

Journey pulled Zion by the arm. She walked him to his car. She kissed him again. She watched as he drove away. She made her way back to the group.

"What the hell was that?"

Shake didn't reply. He took another hit from the blunt. His boys were disappointed. "How you gonna
 let that soft ass nigga play you like that?" One of them asked.

"I'm not sweating that fool. I got business to think about. I can't make paper sitting in jail."

Journey was sick of this life and everything that came with it. She wanted a way out. It was time. She really never thought about leaving, not until this very moment. She headed inside. She slowly took the eight-flight hike. By the time she made it to her floor her heels were killing her feet. She just wanted kick off her shoes and relax on her bed.

"How was the dinner?" Aunt Kelly asked.

Journey smiled. "Nice. It was really nice."

"Oh, Frankie wants to see you. He called earlier."

Journey headed to her room. She was beat mentally. She needed to close her eyes. She climbed into bed still wearing her dress.

"Hey babe. I'm in here."

Zion made his way to the chicken. Beverly was sitting at the table, laptop open and a glass of wine next to her. She motioned for him to have a seat.

"Working?" Zion asked.

"Always. I think it's in my DNA. I don't know how not to."

"So, what do you think?"

"About?"

"Mom lets not play this game. What do you think about Journey?"

She took a sip of her wine then she closed her laptop. She took a deep breath. She leaned back and cleared her throat.

"I'm not sure. I've only spent a couple of hours with her. I could tell that she's a street person. She seems to be respectful. But the question is. What do you think of her?"

Zion was in love. But he couldn't tell his mom how he felt. She would tell him that it's too early, too soon to be in love.

"I like her. She's cool. She's different. She doesn't care about any of this."

Beverly laughs. "She shouldn't, since none of it's hers."

"That was a good one mom."

"I get a good one off every now and then."

"You keep thinking that." Zion said as he kissed his mom on the head and reopened her laptop.

"Back to work lady."

He found his dad sitting up in bed laptop opened sitting in his mom's spot. He was talking on one smart phone and texting on the other. James was all business all the time. He noticed his son standing in the doorway. He waved in. Zion took a seat on the leather sofa at the foot of the bed. James ended his call.

"I didn't think you would be back so soon."

"I have to hit the gym at eight a.m. Then I have a team meeting at noon. "

James checked his incoming message before placing the phone face down.

"Your friend, Journey. Nice girl, and what a looker. I had a thing for edgy girls back in the day."

"Edgy?" Zion asked.

"I guess the correct term is hood these days."

Zion couldn't help but to laugh. There's no way his dad had a thing for girls from the hood. He's way too tight suited.

"Don't laugh. Your old man ran the streets. You better ask somebody. You might not believe it, but before I met your mom. I had this little shorty, with a fat round booty and all of that slick talk."

"So what happened?"

"I upgraded. Shit, your mom is fine as hell. Plus she's a hustler."

"That she is."

"She's a nice girl. Your mom will come around."

Zion gave his dad a hug and then headed to his room to get some shuteye.

Journey couldn't sit still. The four-hour ride to Great Meadow Correctional Facility in Comstock right outside Fort Ann was draining. She wanted to roll up in the hard plastic chair and take a long nap. But she couldn't her mind was racing. Suddenly a large guard who was more fat than muscular told everyone to get inline and to have his or her ID ready.

"Hey Journey." Sandy said.

"Hey."

"I'm really getting too old to make this trip. I'm beat. You just don't know. Lucky for you, you're still young."

"Miss. Sandy I'm getting too old to be making this trip as well. It takes so much out of you."

"The things we do for our love ones. Even when they don't deserve or appreciate it." Journey nodded in agreement. The elderly lady was correct, on both statements. Journey was lead back to a gated waiting area. She could see her brother Frankie sitting at a table. He looked older than the last time she visited.

The guard let her in. She slowly made her way over to Frankie. She could feel eyes on her. Frankie didn't stand to greet her.

"How was the trip?" He asked.

She hated small talk especially with him. She was here for only one reason, so they could discuss business.

"It was long. Long like the last time, and the time before that."

"I heard about your friend."

"He has nothing to do with us."

"That's where you're wrong. He's a distraction. And that distraction is messing with my operation."

"You can't tell me who I can and can't see."

"My word is the same in here as it was out there."

Journey wanted to reach across the table and hit him in the face. It took every bit of her self control not to.

"Oh, I have some information on your friend. Do you even know who his mother is? Well she's the bitch that put me in her. That's right, she's DA Beverly Matthews."

Journey sits in silence.

Frankie said. "Stop seeing him. Or I'm going to reach out and touch him." He stood, before leaving he kissed her on the top of her head. She sat there not knowing what to do. She didn't want to stop seeing him. But she knew her brother would honor his words.

On the bus ride back home she didn't speak to anyone. She placed her headphones on and entered her own little world. She wanted to call Zion. She needed to hear his voice. But that would only make matters worst.

Zion's game was off today. He couldn't throw a rock into the Grand Canyon. His mind was elsewhere.

"You know we barely won that game? What's up?" Derek asked.

Zion lied. "Nothing."

"You're looking for her?"

"Who?"

"Who my ass! You know who. Why don't you go sit on the bench? We can pickup another player. A player with their head in the game."

"My head's in the game. I'm just having a off shooting day."

Palmer said. "We good. You should take a break. You know, take a little time to get focus."

"Man shut up. I'm focused." Zion said taking a seat on the bench. Palmer shook his head in disgust.

"You might as well take your shoes off too. You're done for the day."

Derek called Palmer back to the court. Zion's other teammates didn't say a word. They didn't have to. He knew what they were thinking. Journey entered the park, but she didn't look happy. Zion wanted to rush over and kiss her.

Derek said. "Looks like you got your powers back. You ready to play?" The guys laughed. Zion gave them the bird. Journey took a seat next to him.

"We need to talk."
"Take a ride with me."
"Where are we going?
"Is that a yes?"

Journey leaned back in the passenger seat. The warm thick air ran across her face. She closed her eyes. She didn't want to do it. But she felt that she had no choice.

"Where are we going to?" She asked.

"Edison."

"New Jersey?"

He smiled. She said that she's open to try new things. And this would be something new, at least for her. They pulled into the lot.

"What is this?" She asked.

"Topgolf. I thought hitting some little white balls might relieve your stress."

"Really?"

Journey looked out from the third story bay. The place was amazing. She couldn't believe all the people that were out here on a Sunday hitting golf balls. She never even heard of this place. But she was having a great time. All of her worries had faded away. She was too busy blasting balls out into space.

"You sure you haven't done this before?" Zion asked.

"First time."

"Well look at you."

Journey said. "I'm a natural. Look out Tiger Woods."

"I see you getting your Tiger Hood on."

"You got jokes."

She leaned in and kissed him. She looked deep into his eyes. They were filled with so much joy, so much life and love. She loved him. She loved him more than she wanted to admit to herself or others. Her heart was overflowing with joy and pain, the love that she had for him, and the pain that she had to end this.

On the ride back she didn't say much. She had a ton of things on her mind. Zion took her silence as a sign of being tired. They did have a busy day. And plus he did beat her butt at Topgolf. He didn't want to disturb her, so he remained quite. They pulled up in front of her building. She took a deep a breath. She couldn't look at him. The words wouldn't come out. But they had to, even if she had to pull them out with a rope.

"What's wrong?" He asked.

She shook her head. But she couldn't hide the tears building up in her eyes. He undid his seatbelt. He faced her. "Journey, what's wrong? What's going on?"

She undid her seatbelt. She turned away from him. He pulled her back inside the vehicle.

"What's going on? You can tell me." He pleaded.

"We have to end this. I can't see you again."

Zion's heart fell to his feet. He couldn't believe what his ears were hearing. He was speechless. But he mustered up the strength to ask.

"Why? What's happening here?"

She turned and looked him square in the face. She wiped the tears from her eyes. He said. "What? Why are you doing this?"

"Did you know your mother put my brother in prison for life?"

"I don't know your brother. And my mom's no longer apart of the DA."

"Not now. I have to go. Don't call me again."

Journey slid out of the car. She slammed the door shut. Zion was numb. He couldn't move. He wanted to run after her. But his legs wouldn't obey his brain. He watched as she raced into her building. He slowly put his car in drive and then pulled off heading for home.

He headed right to his room. He fell on the bed. He didn't know what to do. He's never been in love before. The hurt came fast and hard. He wanted to know what went wrong, and what did his mother have to do with it. He called Derek.

"What's good son? I just want you to know we got smashed. I had to go back to the crib early. Palmer played like shit. I hope you had fun though."

"She ended it."

Derek was confused. "End what?"

"She said that she could no longer see me."

Derek wasn't too shocked. Journey and his cousin come from two totally different worlds. Zion no matter how cool he is. He will never understand the street life. And journey will never be a socialite no matter how you clean her up.

"I'm sorry to hear that. But I'm not surprise."

"What does that mean?" Zion shot back.

"I know Journey, and I know you. It wasn't a match made in heaven."

"Really?"

"Don't take it like that fam. I'm just saying. You don't fit in her world, and she sure doesn't fit in yours."

Zion knew that it would be hard to mesh their worlds together. But he believed that they could. He wanted to give it a shot.

"Did she say why?"

"Something about mom putting her brother in prison. But I think it's something more. Something she can't tell me."

"Don't dig too hard fam. Those niggas will dead you. It's not worth it. They're on some different shit. You feel me?"

"This can't be real. Man, I'm just trying to figure out what happened.

"Let it be." Derek said.

"You might be right. I'm going to get off of here. I'll get with you soon."

"Peace fam."

Zion turned off his cell. He pitched to the top of his dresser. He kicked off his shoes. He wanted to call Journey. But instead he headed to the kitchen where he found his mom eating a slice of lemon cake. He grabbed a fork and joined her.

"How was your night?" She asked.

"Not so good."

She took a small piece of the cake with her fork. She glanced over at her son. He didn't look so good.

"Journey?"

"How did you know?"

"A man has a certain look when his pain involves a woman."

"She said we shouldn't see each other."

Beverly ate as she listened. She's been here before growing up in a house with two younger brothers.

"What was her reason?"

"She really didn't say, other than you put her brother in jail."

"Maddox?"

"Yes."

Beverly placed her fork on the island. She took a sip of her milk.

"I do recall a Maddox, a drug case, a large amount of drugs if I recall correctly. I think the judge threw the book at him. So that was her brother?"

"I guess so."

"What does that have to do with you? That case was over ten years ago."

"I wanted to asked her that. But the words wouldn't come out."

James enters the room. He grabs a beer from the fridge.

"Can I join or is this a private conversation?"

Beverly said. "Girl trouble."

"As long as you have a girl in your life there will be trouble."

"Really?" Beverly said.

"What's the problem kiddo?"

Zion didn't want to go into it again. It was too much to bare to hear those words again. He just wanted to eat the cake and call it a night.

"Nothing, but thanks for the concern. I'm heading off."

"Good night son." Beverly said. He gave his mom a kiss and dad a hug. He finished off the cake before retiring.

James said. "What's going on?"

Beverly cut herself another slice of the delicious lemon cake. James took a seat next to her. He wanted to share her slice. She waved him off.

"Cut you some."

"I don't want a full slice. I just want a taste."

She motioned him to get his own cake. He decided that cake and beer wasn't such a great mix.

"Tell me what's happening with our son."

"Apparently I was the DA in her brother's case."

"You won."

"You know I did." She said with a laugh

James didn't want to dig any deeper. He could tell this was a touchy subject. Beverly was like a momma bear when it came to her children.

"When you finish I'll be in the bedroom."

"Is that an invitation for sex?" She asked.

"I'll see you in the bedroom."

Zion sat at his desk editing a video from his latest Lifevantage presentation. He had to do something to keep his mind off Journey. He wanted to call her so badly. But he had to honor her wish, that's what a gentleman would do.

He turned off his computer, and his cell phone. He took a quick shower and then headed to bed.

Journey joined her nephews at the small kitchen table. The box of cereal was empty; the milk was gone as well. She didn't have any cash to go to the store, everything they had went to the connect. They were broke. Aunt Kelly won't get paid until Friday. And her mom's food stamps are gone.

She fell onto the sofa. The remote on the other side of the room, she didn't want to get up to get it. But what other choice did she have? Just then there was knock at the door. Aunt Kelly answered the door. Journey knew that the voice. The voice made her heart skip a beat, her hands got sweaty.

"Journey, you have a visitor."

Zion entered the small apartment. His bedroom seemed bigger. Journey was happy to see him. She couldn't hide her smile. But she knew this was a bad idea.

"What are you doing here?" She asked.

"I had to see you."

She introduced Zion to her family. Her mom was out, not of the house, but out from a night of drinking. Journey lead Zion out to the hallway. He pulled her close. They kissed. He felt energized. She felt fear.

Zion said. "I need you. You're the best thing that has happened to me."

"I…"

"…I'm not giving up." He told her.

"There's so much that you don't know. That you won't understand."

He pulled her close once again. He didn't want to let her go. He couldn't breath without her. She held him tight. But she had to let him go.

"You shouldn't be here."

"I had to see you. You're in my system."

She kissed him, and then she slowly pushed him away. She couldn't look him in the eyes as she went into her apartment. It took all of his might not to kick in the door and kiss her one last time.

Palmer waves the waitress over. She's cute, and just his type, young and dumb. She flirts with him. She has a knack for knowing when guys or even some girls are into her.

"How are you doing this evening beautiful?"

She flashes a fake smile. Zion laughs. Palmer believes his game is on. He's pulling out the big guns now. He pulls out a hundred dollar bill, hands it to the waitress.

"I can tell that your service is going to be A1."

"Can you now?" She takes the C-Note, thanks him and continues to take their order.

"That's for you sweetie." Palmer states.

"I thought so." She said as she continued to take notes. Zion didn't mind that Palmer wasn't paying him any attention. He was more interested in getting the waitress's number. Zion just wanted to be out of the house. He needed to do something, anything to get Journey out of his head.

"I thought you said four o'clock Palmer." Derek said as he took a seat next to Zion.

"I did. Zion said he was already on his way out. I just forgot to call you. But you're here now, so no foul." Derek shook his head in disgust. Palmer has an excuse for everything. The young waitress strolled over.

"Would you like a menu?"

Derek smiled. She smiled back. Derek was more her taste. Her smile was big and bright. She was easy on the eyes.

"No thank you. I know what I want."

"And what is that?" She asked never taking her eyes off of him.

"I'll have a turkey sandwich and a small coke."

"Is that all?"

"For now." He said.

Zion stared out the window. He couldn't shake the thought of being without Journey. He checked his phone, for what reason? She wasn't going to call and he knew it.

Derek asked. "How's the parents, oh and your big headed sister?"

"Everyone is fine. And I'm going to tell Zoe what you said."

"Good, I want you to."

Palmer couldn't believe that his waitress was flirting with Derek. He had more going for himself than Derek. Hell didn't she see the Benz he pulled up in? And Derek took an Uber. She had to be off of her nut.

"So what's happening with your situation?" Derek asked just as the waitress returned with his order. Zion didn't want to talk about it. He changed the subject.

"You balling Sunday?" He asked.

"No doubt. You coming out Palmer?"

Palmer sipped his drink as he eyed the waitress. Derek motioned toward Palmer. Zion laughed. Palmer mentally came back to the group.

"What? What's up?" He asked.

"Just ask her for her number."

Palmer thought about it. Zion was right. He should just come out and ask for her number. What could she say other than no?

"I'll be back." Palmer said.

Zion and Derek watched as Palmer made his way over to the counter. Zion wasn't so sure if it was a good idea after all. Derek on the other hand was thrilled to see his friend go for it.

"I would like to say I'm sorry for our last talk. I was out of line. I should have been there for you. We are family."

"I understand your point of view. I just didn't want to hear it at the time. But you were clearly right."

Palmer returned with a defeated look. The guys had a good laugh. Not so funny to Palmer. They paid their bill and then went their separate ways. Derek hopped in with Zion.

Derek turned down the radio. He wanted to speak with his cousin. He really didn't know where to start.

"Like I said, I'm sorry I wasn't there for you."

Zion smiled. He could never stay upset with his cousin and best friend.

"Man, it's all good. We're good, don't worry about it."

Zion turned the music up. They nodded their heads as they rode through the city. They flirted with girls along the way. Zion played along. He had to get over Journey. They headed over to Columbus Circle to window shop.

Derek said. "You ready to get back to school?"

"Yes and no. I have a big work load this year."

Not paying attention Zion bumps into a group of guys. It turns out to be Shake and his crew. Derek knew this could be trouble.

Zion said. "I'm sorry. I didn't see you."

"You are sorry. Sorry ass nigga. Watch where you're going."

Zion said. "Like I said, my bad. All that tough talk we really don't need."

Shake's ready to end this. But he's not willing to square up. He's a gunplay kind of a guy. Derek nods to the group. He pulls his cousin by the arm.

Shake said. "You better move along with Dee, before you get laid out."

Zion may have been born with a silver spoon, but he's no coward. Money doesn't erase his skin color. He's had to fight his whole life. If it wasn't the white kids at his schools, it was the kids in the hood whenever he went to visit Derek.

"Like I said before, Shook, Shake or whatever your name maybe. You can step up and get knocked out anytime."

"Damn! This nigga got big monster balls. You gonna let this nigga play you like that?"

Shake wanted to shut Zion's mouth, but not here. There were too many eyes. But he was going to reach out and touch this nigga. Zion's day was coming.

The group parted. Zion slowly followed Derek. He wanted to put his fist through Shake's chest. Shake was too old to be fighting twenty year olds.

"Fam, we're out numbered."

"Those guys can't fight, that's why they all carry guns." Zion said.

"That's why you walk away. They all got guns."

"They're not going to shoot up the mall in the middle of the day, they're not that gangster."

Derek said. "I hope you're right."

Journey exited the building. The sun warmed her face. She crossed the street and headed for the subway. Just then a black SUV pulled up next to her. The window went down. Miguel smiled at her. She knew what this was all about. Her first thought was to run. But where would she run. There was nowhere to go that the cartel couldn't find her.

Miguel said. "Take a ride with me."

She knew this could be it; this could be the last ride that she would ever take. She scanned the area.

"I'm not asking."

"I'm in a rush." She said.

"I can drop you wherever you're rushing to."

She didn't have a choice. She climbed in. Miguel got right to it.

"My boss isn't happy. You're short, real short."

Journey said. "I don't understand. Everyone paid. It was all there. We had to delay paying the crews because of this rush you have us under."

"Are you calling me a liar?" Miguel asked.

Journey knew she had to choose her words carefully if she wanted to make it out of here with her life.

"Not at all. I'll look into it."

"You have sticky fingers in your operation."

"How short?" She asked.

Miguel took out his Note 9, then the pen. He wrote a number on the screen. He passed the phone over to Journey. She swallowed hard. It was a big number.

"You have five days to get the rest of our money."

Miguel motioned for the driver to pull over. Journey was in a tough spot. There was no way she could come up with that number in five days.

"I hope this is a good spot." Miguel said.

"It's cool."

"I'll see you in five days"

"Sure."

She stood at the corner watching the SUV move down the street. What was she going to do? She was broke. All of her stash money was gone. She had to use it to make the drop. She had to call the crews. They had to move the rest of the product. She texted the crews, it was time for a face to face.

Derek and Zion rested on the iron-gate outside of Derek's building. Zion's phone went off. He checked it. He didn't recognize the number.

"I bet that's Aunt Beverly telling you to make it home for dinner."

"That's only on Sundays. And speaking of Sunday, it's been a minute since you had Sunday dinner with us."

"I'm down if your pop's making that killer ass meatloaf."

"I'll see what I can do." Zion said.

"Don't just see what you can do. I need that. You need to jump on that ASAP."

Zion noticed two guys headed in their direction. It was nothing to be concerned about since people were constantly in and out. Zion turned his attention back to his cousin. The fear in Derek's eyes told him all he needed to know. As soon as he turned to face the men the flash blinded him. Derek ran; Zion did the same, but in the opposite direction.

He could hear each gun shot followed by screams. He prayed that Derek was safe. He knew that the guys were there for him. He ran. He ran as fast as he could. He ran until there were no longer any shots fired. He checked his pockets. He pulled his cell out.

He called Derek, but there was no answer. He wanted to backtrack. But what if the shooters were counting on that.

He called again. This time Derek picked up.

"Hey man, are you okay?"

Derek said. "I'm good. What about you?"

"I'm okay." He said. And then a sharp pain ran through his body. His shirt was wet. He looked down. His shirt was covered in blood.

"Oh man. I'm hit."

"What do you mean you're hit?"

Zion placed his hand over his wound. The pressure should slow the bleeding. He thought about trying to make it back to his vehicle.

Zion said. "I'm shot, and it hurts like a son of a bitch. I need to get to a hospital."

"I'm calling your parents." Derek said.

He called his Aunt Beverly, but she didn't pick up. He scanned the area. The shooters were gone. He called his Uncle James. Before he could tell his Uncle what has taken place the police were on the scene. He ran over to the officers.

"My cousin was shot. He's over here. The shooters ran that way."

The officers made their way around the building. They found Zion sitting in the corner. He had his car keys in his hand and his cell phone in the other. His face was cover with sweat. The officer called for an ambulance. Zion dropped his keys. He placed his shaking hand over the bleeding hole in his side.

The officer asked. "Do you know who did this?"

Zion knew that Shake had something to do with it. But he didn't recognize the triggermen.

"I don't."

The officer shook his head. People in this part of town seem to never know who or why they end up the victim.

"I don't know who they were. I don't even live over here." He told the officer.

"Well someone wanted you dead. Sit tight, we have a bus on the way."

Beverly stormed in the room, James and Zoe in tow. Derek and his mom were sitting in the corner. Beverly went right to her baby. She kissed him and held him tight.

James asked. "What happened?"

"We were sitting out front and out of nowhere two guys starting shooting."

Beverly cut him off. "Were they shooting at you two?"

Zion didn't speak. He didn't want to lie. It was best that he stayed tight lipped.

"I don't know." Derek answered. "We hear the shots and ran for cover."

"Where's your doctor?"

"Mom he'll be in shortly."

James gave Derek and his a mom a big hug. He was happy that no one was hurt or worst, killed.

"Are you alright?" He asked.

"Yes Sir. I'm good."

Zoe took a seat next to her Aunt. It's been ages since they've seen one another. Ever since her ex-husband, Derek's father went to jail they've lost touch. She doesn't blame anyone for moving on with their lives. She's happy that Derek is so close to them and Zion.

The doctor strolls in. His hair is a mess, not to mention he has a coffee stain on his tie. Beverly is a stickler for the details.

"You must be Zion's folks. Well like I explained to his Aunt, the bullet went straight through."

Beverly asked. "Meaning?"

"There's no damage to any vital organs. He's one lucky musketeer."

"Thank you. How soon will he be able to come home? James asked.

"I would give it a day. I would like to keep him here overnight just to keep an eye on him."

Beverly said. "You just stated that he was fine."

"Yes, and fine he is. But it's never a bad idea to play things on the safe side."

"I'm staying." Beverly announced.

"I can stay."

"No, you go. I have my laptop, so I can do some work while he rest. Plus you have an early morning. We can call for a car tomorrow."

Zoe said. I can stay too."

"Nice try. But you have practice tomorrow."

"Missing one day isn't going to improve my game."

Zion said. "That's true."

"You're so funny. How did they miss that big head of yours?"

"Don't ever say anything like that again." Beverly told her.

James mentioned for Zoe to get her belongings.

"I can drop you off." James told Derek and his mom.

Everyone exited the room, everyone except James and Beverly. James moved closer to his son. He took his hand. There was so much he wanted to say. But the words wouldn't come out. He squeezed his son's hand.

James said. "I'm so thankful that you're alright."

"Dad, I'm good. I am."

"I know. But you need to know. You mean the world to me. You and your sister, you're my world. I love you."

"I love you dad."

"I'm going to walk down with them. I have to grab my bag. But I won't be long." She said.

"No rush mom. I'm good."

Journey leads back in her seat. Shake sits across form her. The place is packed with runners. They're bagging up, but the product is short, not enough to make up the difference of what is owed.

"I don't think we're going make it." Journey said.

Shake took a long drag off of his New Port. "That's the natural of the beast."

"The beast is going to get us all killed." Journey told him. She motioned for him to put out the smoke. He took a long drag before doing so. She wanted to say something about the missing money, but she didn't know whom she could trust.

"I need you to call all the outlets. We need the money upfront on this next shipment."

"Journey, that's not going to happen, we both know that."

"Make it happen. I'm sure Miguel has shooters
on stand by."

Shake didn't care. He wasn't going to call any of the crews. He had a plan. And it didn't include Journey or the business.

"I got you." He told her.

Journey gathered her belongings. She had to make it home before her mom headed out to drink. The boys would be home all alone.

"I'll be in touch." She said before leaving.

Journey exited the subway train. The platform was crowded. She made her way down to the street. A kid from the block waved her over.

89

"Hey Journey, what's good?" He asked.

"Same shit son."

"You got a smoke?"

"I'm fresh out." She told him.

"Did you hear about Derek? Some niggas ran up on him and some other nigga and just started blasting."

She couldn't believe her ears. Her heart dropped. Her feet wouldn't move. It was like she was standing in cement.

"What happened?" she asked.

"I don't know. I don't know if they got shot or killed or anything."

Journey hurried off. She needed to know if Zion was okay. She called him, but it went right to voicemail. She panic, she ran over to Derek's. She banged on the door.

"Who is it?" Derek asked.

"It's me. It's Journey."

The door swung open. She slowly entered. The place was spotless, nothing fancy, but clean. Derek yelled out from the kitchen.

Journey closed the door, and then headed to kitchen.

"What are you doing here?" He asked.

"I heard what happened. Are you okay? Is Zion alright?"

Derek laughed. "I knew you weren't here to see on me."

"I'm here. I was worried about you, you and Zion." She said as she took the wooden spoon from Derek and started to stir the soup. He loved her hands. Her fingers were long and thin.

Derek said. "I miss you."

"Derek, we're still friends. That hasn't changed."

"Everything changed once you joined the family business."

"I didn't come here to talk about that."

"Why don't you go to the hospital? That's where you want to be."

"So it's like that?"

"Journey its been like that. I haven't heard from you in years. You come to the court and act like we were never close."

"Derek, you're making a mountain out of an ant hill." She told him. She placed the spoon on the counter.

"I think it's best that I leave. What hospital is he in?"

"Call his folks. Bye Journey."

Journey closed the door as she exited. She wanted to tell him to go to hell. But that would have been anger speaking and not her true feelings. She loved Derek, they been friends forever. But he was correct; things changed once she got older and joined the business.

She pulled her cell from her backpack. She had Zion on speed dial. The phone rung, and rung, and then went to voicemail. She called Zoe.

"Hey Journey. What's up?"

"How's Zion? I just heard."

"He's fine. He was shot, but he's okay. Mom stayed with him."

"I called but he didn't pick up."

Zoe told her. "You're on his shit list. But I'm going to send you the address."

"Thanks."

Journey stood outside his door contemplating if coming here was a smart decision. Just as she decided to leave she got a message. It was from Zoe. It read, "Don't punk out." Journey smiled. What the hell? She's here, might as well go in.

She slowly pushed the door open. Zion was sitting up in bed watching ESPN. Zion glanced over. He tried to hide his joy.

"What brings you here?" He asked.

She came close. She leaned against the iron rail of the bed. She removed her small backpack.

"Derek told me what happened. Are you okay?"

"I was shot. But other than that I guess I'm okay." He searched for the remote. She smiled. It was sitting in his lap.

"You looking for this?" She asked as she handed it to him. He was happy to see her. She always made things better at least it felt that way to him.

"Hey babe this is all I could find." Beverly said as he entered the room carrying a tuna salad sandwich purchased from the cafeteria machine.

"Oh, I didn't realize you had company."

"Hello." Journey said in a low soft voice. She knew breaking the heart of a mother's son was a no no. She was standing behind the plate with one strike, for now.

"Hello. How have you been?"

"Busy. I ran into Derek. He told me what had happened."

Beverly placed the cold sandwich in front of Zion. She then returned to her seat. She opened her Macbook and continued to work.

"Mom, could you give us a minute?"

Beverly closed her laptop. She slowly got to her feet and then strolled out of the room. She stood in the hallway as she waited.

"What?" Journey asked.

"I take it that you don't know."

Journey took a seat next to him on the bed. He moved over to make room.

She said. "What are you talking about?"

"Shake did this."

She hopped off of the bed. It couldn't be so. She didn't believe it. Shake had to get the green light from above before he could take out anyone.

"Why would you say that?" She asked.

"Him and I had words earlier today. I guess it's an coincidence that guys came gunning for me a few hours later."

"I'll look into it. But I think you're wrong."

"Yeah." He turned up the television. He didn't care to hear her excuses. Journey stood there not wanting to believe it.

"I have to go." She told him.

"Later."

Journey adjusted her bag. She turned to leave, then she looked back. Zion was focused on the boob tube. She exited the room. Beverly stopped her.

"Do you know who did this to my son?"

"I don't." She said.

"I hope that's true. I have friends in very high places, friends who don't take kindly to this kind of thing."

Journey didn't respond. She politely stepped around Beverly and left the building. She stood in the hospital parking lot wondering if Shake really had something to with the attack. She knew that Zion and him weren't ever going to be friends. But would he do such a thing? And if he did, the order came from the top, her brother Frankie.

She exited the Uber. She headed right for her building. Po and Lee stopped her.

"What good Journey?" Po asked.

"Not a thing. Have you seen Shake?"

"Naw, but his number two said that we short, real short and the top guy wants his paper."

Lee said. "I'm not trying to get kill cus y'all short."

"Nigga, we're short. You knew the rules when you joined the family. Don't bitch up now. Ain't none of this shit brand new."

"You right. You right." Lee said.

Journey said. "I'm out. We're going to make it right with the connect."

Journey strolled into her building. The staircase was crammed with thugs, some working their hustle, others just wasting time. When they saw her they cleared a path. She walked the eight flights to her floor. She milled over the thought of her brother placing a hit on Zion. She had to found out for herself.

She entered the apartment; her nephews were on the floor playing a video game.

"Where's your mom?" She asked.

"She went out with some friends. Granny's not here either."

She figured as much. Her mom never wanted to be home. She never wanted kids, and she let them know it every chance she got.

Zion took a seat next to Zoe at the kitchen table. She nodded. He smiled. He loved his little sister with all of his heart.

"Where are the parents?" He asked.

"Work."

"Work?

"Yes, work. You've been out for the past two days."

"What are you doing?"

"Checking my social media. You know I'm something like a star."

Zion slapped her phone from her hand. "Sure you are."

"You're lucking you didn't break my phone. I just got this thing."

"I'm going to take a shower. Has anyone called since I've been out?"

"No, Journey hasn't called. But Derek stopped by yesterday."

"Okay."

# Three

Journey stood at the edge of the door scanning the hallway. Her time was up and she didn't have the money. Shake and other members of the family have been laying low, not returning her calls. She had to hit the streets to see what was what. She slowly exited. She thought about taking the elevator, but then ruled it out.

She made to the lobby. It was too early for the young thugs to be out. She made it out to the courtyard. The coast was clear. She hurried to the subway. It felt like everyone was watching her. She made it to the platform. She tried to stay out of the crowd. A large crowd would make her easy pickings for a hit man.

She received a text. It read "Time's up." She didn't reply. The text said everything. The doors opened and she rushed into the car. She took a seat next to an old man. She positioned herself so she could see the whole subway car. As she got closer to her stop she noticed an older

Mexican man standing close to the door. He tried to act as if he wasn't watching her. The train came to a stop. She stood up to exit the train. The Mexican gentleman stepped out onto the platform and waited. Journey took her time exiting the car. The doors started to close. She stepped back into the car. The man smiled. She winked.

She took her phone out of bag. She pitched it out the window. How else could he have located her? She got off at the next stop. She ran to the spot. Lee and Po were standing out front.

"What's wrong with you?" Lee asked.

"Have you seen Shake?"

"What's up? He's inside."

"Come inside. I can't be standing out in the open."

Lee followed her inside. She closed the door behind them. She fell hard into the iron chair.

"Miguel sent someone to kill me." She said.

"What?"

"He sent someone to kill me. He was on the subway."

"Someone tried to kill you on the subway?"

"Yes and no."

"Shit, we need to tool up." Shake said.

"I need to get in touch with my brother. I'm sure Miguel has people on the inside."

"Shit if he sent someone for you, then you know he's going for Frankie."

"Right?" Lee said.

"Fuck! I'm out. I can't be sitting around waiting to get my head cut off. You know how those Mexicans do."

"I need to get word to Frankie."

"Good luck with that. You better roll with us. You don't want to be caught out here alone." Lee told her.

Le was right. There was no way she could go up against a professional killer. There's safety in numbers.

"Let me grab a burner and I'll meet you outside." Journey told him.

"Don't take too long or you'll be on your own."

Shake exited the room. He told his boys to be on alert. He wasn't going down without a fight. He needed to get out of town. His plan was to drop Journey off and then head right to Union Station. He told Lee to go back inside and light a fire under Journey's ass. She was taking too long and time wasn't on their side.

A rusted out van pulled up to Journey's building. It stopped and then the side door slid back. Journey stepped out, so did Po and Lee. Shake slammed the door close. The van pulled off leaving the three of them standing under the street light.

Po said. "I'm ghost."

"I'm out to." Lee told her.

Just as she turned to head in, someone called out her name. She knew that voice. She was happy to hear that voice. She turned and there he stood. She ran to him. She jumped into his arms. They kissed.

"We have to get out of here." She said.

"Anywhere you want to go."

They drove for hours. She wanted to be on the move. She can't stand still, not even for a second. Zion pulled into a station.

"What are you doing?" She asked.

Zion turned the car off. He shifted his body so he was facing her. "What's going on?"

"It's not your concern."

"Journey, what's going on? I may be able to help. But we'll never know if you don't open up to me."

He was right. How could they move forward if she didn't let him in? But this was something different.

"I'm dead."

Zion leaned in closer. If this was a joke it's not funny. "What are you talking about? What do you mean you're dead?"

"I have someone trying to kill me." She told him.

"What?"

"We owe the Sinaloa Cartel a large amount of money." She told him.

"How much do you owe?" He asked.

"Two hundred thousand. But it doesn't matter. I'm dead."

"Don't say that. There has to be something we can do."

"You got two hundred K you can loan me?" She said half kidding. If he had it, she would have it. But they were both out of luck. He readjusted his body. He turned on the car.

"I might know someone who could help." Zion said as he pulled off.

Palmer poured himself a hard drink. Zion was his best friend, but he was asking for a lot here. Two hundred isn't a small order. He had to run it over in his head.

Palmer said. "I need five percent on my investment."

"Okay." Zion said.

"I'm not sure if Miguel will even take it." Zion told her. "Call and ask."

Journey was scared to make the call. She didn't what to hear what Miguel had to say. That's if he would even pick up.

"It's not that easy." She said

"It is." He said pulling her close. He hands her his cell phone. "Make the call."

She places his phone on the table. She pulls her burner from her bag. Miguel has a high tech team of trackers. She doesn't want to give away her location. The phone rings. The voice on the other end said hello in Spanish.

"Hola." Journey said. "It's Journey, Necesito hablar con el jefe"

The phone went silent. She thought they hung up. Miguel spoke into the phone. "You don't have our money. You know what that means?"

"I have it. It just took a little longer. But I have it."

"You do? How? You didn't have the time to sell enough product to do so."

"I found a way." She told him.

"I'm surprised, and impressed at the same time."

"I need two hours, then we can meet. I'll name the location."

"You don't trust me?" He asked.

"Two hours." She told him. And then she hung up.

Zion couldn't believe that he was mixed up in Cartel business. He thanked Palmer for his help.

"Why didn't you just give her the money? I know you have it." Palmer said.

"I don't have it in cash. Plus the transfer would take too long. Not to mention my parents."

"I understand. But this is money. So I have to keep it real with you."

"I wouldn't except anything less."

"Zion, we have to go." She told him.

"I'll get this back to you in a few weeks." He told palmer.

"With interest."

"I hear you man. I got you covered."

Journey called Miguel. She wanted to get this over with as soon as she could. She's never thought of leaving the family business before, but now she wasn't so sure this was for her any longer. At this moment she decided that she wanted more. This was it for her.

Zion pulled into the parking lot.

"I'm going in, alone."

There was no way he was going to let her go in there without back up. He didn't know what he could do, but she wasn't going in alone.

"Zion, it's best that they don't know who you are. Once they get dug in, they dig deep."

"I don't want you to go in by yourself." He said.

"That's sweet. But this isn't new to me. I can handle this."

She exited the car. She pulled the gym bag filled with cash from the backseat. Zion watched as she went into the diner. He turned on the radio as he prepared to wait it out.

Journey strolled over to counter. Miguel waved her over to his booth. He motioned for her to have a seat.

"Is that the money?" Miguel asked.

"It is."

"You showed me something. You don't break under pressure. We could use someone like you to take over your brother's operation."

"I don't understand."

"Under his watch, things have been, not as smooth. Plus we need someone on the streets. We need someone with, lets say, their boots on the ground."

"I don't think so. Starting now, at this very moment. I'm out. I'm done with this life."

"But you're not." You still have some of our product. We want our money. We can circle back to this conversation at a later date."

He waved over the waitress. He asked. "Would you like a cup of coffee?"

"No thanks."

Miguel ordered a cup of coffee, black. The waitress looked at Journey.

"I'm good, thank you." The waitress left.

"I'm done with this live. What are you going to do, kill me? I don't care. I'm done."

"We won't kill you. But we'll definitely kill Frankie, you mother, you Aunt and her sons."

"I love them. But I'm no longer doing this. So take your money and fuck off."

Miguel said. "Give me the bag."

She slid it over to him with her foot. A large Mexican man sitting at the counter came over and took the bag. Journey watched as he went out to the waiting black SUV.

"Oh, or maybe we'll kill lover boy sitting out there. There's not much we don't know about you or your circle of friends."

"You can do what you want. But I'm out."

"Where's your right hand?" He asked.

"I believe he went underground. I can't locate him."

Miguel laughs. She knew that laugh. He knew something. He was dying for her to inquire.

"What's so funny?" She asked.

"I've located him." Journey didn't care. She was done with this life.

"I know his exact location at this moment." Miguel said. The tall Mexican gentleman returned. He dropped a piece of paper on the table before taking his seat back at the counter. Miguel glanced at the note.

"It's all there." He said.

"You have your money. We're done here. You have a pleasant trip back to Mexico." She went to exit the booth. The tall guy blocked her exit.

"Take a ride with me." Miguel said.

"I don't think so." She answered.

"Don't you want to see your friend Shake?"

"No. As far as I'm concern. I'm done with him as well. Move your guy before I start screaming my head off."

Miguel couldn't afford a scene. He shouldn't even be in the states. Miguel waved his man away.

"Good day to you Journey."

"Bye Miguel."

She exited the dinner and jumped into Zion's car. They sped away so quick that Miguel couldn't place a tail on them. The waitress retuned with his coffee. He sent word that the payment was paid in full. He didn't mention the situation with Journey.

Zion pulled into the driveway. He put the vehicle in park. He removed his seatbelt.
"Why are we here?" She asked.
"I wanted you to be somewhere safe."
"Your mom's not a fan of mine. I'm not so sure you can call this a safe place."
"Everyone's in Miami. I have the place all to myself."
"I can't stay."
He told her. "I believe you can. And you will."
"I can, doesn't mean I will."

Journey woke to the sun shining bright. The small alarm clock read 1:45pm. She couldn't believe that she slept so long. But it was a much-needed rest. The room was big, the bed was super comfortable, it was like sleeping on clouds. She noticed that her clothes neatly folded and resting on a chair in the corner. She realized that she was wearing someone else's shorts and tee shirt.

The door slowly opened. Zion peeked his head in. She waved. He took his time entering the room.

"How did you sleep?" He asked.

"Like a baby."

"You want some lunch?"

She asked. "Who took my clothes off? I don't remember taking my clothes off. Is this your sister's room."

"Guest room. We had a long night. My tee, my mom's shorts."

"Really?"

"I took the liberty of washing you clothes. I hope you don't mind. I cooked. The rest room is in there. I'll be in the kitchen."

Journey told him she would be out soon. She closed the door and then skipped to the bathroom. She found Zion sitting at the kitchen table.

"What do we have here?" She asked.

"Chipotle Chicken Lettuce Wraps and freshly squeezed lemonade."

"Well look at you."

"I try." He said.

After lunch they spent a little time on the patio. Journey knew she couldn't stay here forever, but she didn't want to leave.

"What now?" He asked.

"I'm not sure. Miguel said that he had Shake. I have to contact my people."

Zion didn't care if Shake was in the hands of the cartel, he believed that Shake gave the order to kill him. But Shake was a part of Journey's crew. No matter how much he didn't like him, he would still help Journey to locate him. And then he would give him an old fashion beating.

"I need a shower." She said.

He led her to his bathroom. He grabbed a clean towel and washcloth. The bathroom was beautiful, too nice for a guy in his early twenties.

"Your mom did a nice job."

"Actually it was my dad. He designed the whole place from top to bottom."

"You need to get out so I can undress. Unless you're going to join me."

Was it really about to happen? He couldn't believe it. He's been waiting for this moment. She laughs.

"I'm kidding. Did you really think I would have sex in your parents home?"

He had to think about it. "Get out." She told him.

Zion put on a fresh pair of clothes. He waited for Journey to exit the bathroom. She had a bright white towel wrapped around her.

"My clothes. You forgot to bring me my clothes."

"Oh." He hurried to the guest room retrieve her garments. When he returned the towel was on the floor. She was standing there wearing nothing other than her smile. He waited her. All he ever wanted was her. From the first day they met he was in love.

"Are you just going to stand there with your mouth open or are you going to bring me my clothes?"

Okay, maybe things weren't playing out the way he imagined.

"Do you always tease?"

"I'm not. Just showing you what could be yours."

"Could be?"

Journey jumped into her clothes. She pulled her locks back into a ponytail. Zion picked up his keys from the kitchen counter. They raced out the door.

"Where are we going? He asked.

"To check some of our lay low spots. We have a few so it might take some time. You good with that?"

Zion didn't have anything better to do. But his heart wasn't in it. He didn't care for Shake.

He wanted to be with her. They went to every known location, each time she was disappointed. Maybe Miguel knew where Shake was, because he had him. And if he had him, he was already dead.

"Take me home"

Zion glanced over. She didn't take her eyes off of the road. She felt sad. She wanted to cry, but not in front of Zion. She knew he wouldn't understand. As bad as Shake was, he was like family to her.

"Are you sure?" He asked.

"I am. I have to look in on my family."

"I can go with you."

"You've done enough." She told him.

The car pulled to the curb, she jumped out. She bent down and smiled. He could see the worry on her face. But he said nothing.

"I'll call you later." She told him.

"Okay."

He watched as she raced passed the crowd and into the building. He made the decision not to go after her. Is she safe? That's all he could think about on his way home. He gripped the steering wheel so tight that his hands started to hurt. He pulled into the driveway and then turned the car off. His legs were numb. His mouth was dry. He thought about going back.

But Journey didn't want that. He must obey her wishes, no matter how much he disagreed. He went inside. He headed right to his room. He fell onto bed without turning on the light.

Journey entered the apartment to find her family all sitting in the front room. The television was on, but no one seems to be really watching it.

She asked. "What's going on?"

The door slowly closed behind her. She turned and there stood the Mexican man from the subway. He held what looked like a Glock 19 or 23 fitted with a small compressor. Journey moved away from the door. Her mom pulled her close.

"I paid Miguel." She said.

"I'm waiting for a call. So please shut up."

Journey took a seat on the arm of the second hand sofa. She told her nephews that everything would be all right. They had nothing to fear.

The Mexican man leaned on the door. His finger resting on the trigger, he wanted to pull it. But he had to first get the okay from his employer.

His cell phone rung, he slowly placed it to his ear. He didn't speak. He ended the call and then returned the phone to his pocket. He opened the door and then exited without saying a word.

"Really Journey? You trying to get us all killed?" Her mom screamed. Journey went to her room. She grabbed a small bag from the closet.

"What are you doing?" Aunt Kelly asked.

"I'm out."

"Where will you go?" She asked taking a seat on the bed.

"I don't know."

"Why don't you sleep on it? We all had a rough day."

Aunt Kelly exited the room. Journey fell onto the bed. She needed to call Zion, but not now.

She had to get out of the city. What if Miguel changes his mind, and wants her dead?

She woke up the next morning to her mom calling her to the front room. She didn't want to move. She didn't care what was happening in the other room.

"Journey get your skinny ass in here." Her mom yelled.

She rolled off of the bed. She dragged herself into the front room. Aunt Kelly and her mom were standing in front of the television.

"What's so important?" She asked.

"Look."

The local reporter was at the Brooklyn Bridge. It seemed to be the location of some kind of crime. The reporter stated that the authorities first thought this could have been a suicide, but once they discovered that the body's hands have been removed they ruled that out.

Journey knew that it was Shake. She didn't see the body since they wouldn't show it on the tube. But she knew, deep down inside she knew it was him. The removing of the hands was a sign to point out he was a thief.

Just then she thought about her brother. But there was nothing she or anyone on the outside could do. She went back to her room to finish packing.

Zion sat at the table with his family. They returned late last night. He didn't say much. All he could think about was Journey. He wanted to call her. But he didn't have the number to her burner.

Dad was checking he news when he came across the hanging at the bridge. Bel moved in to get a closer look.

"What is this world coming to?" She asked.

"What it's always been." Dad answered.

Zoe finished her breakfast and then cleaned up her eating area. She motioned to her mom it was time to head out.

"Young lady don't rush me."

"Mom, you know coach makes us run if we're late."

Beverly picked up her keys from the counter. She kisses James and then Zion before following Zoe out to the garage.

"What's your plans for the day?" James asked.

Zion took his time finishing his meal. He didn't have any plans. He wanted to see Journey. But he couldn't just show up unannounced.

"I have a meeting with my team at one o'clock at Starbuck's."

"I'm going to be late tonight. I have to go Philly to look at some property. Your mom knows, but I wanted to keep you in the loop."

"I am sort of the man of the house when you're not here." Zion said.

"Sort of, you're something like the man of the house when I'm away."

Zion smiled. He loved being his father's son. He's more like his old man than he would care to admit. He killed off his apple juice before placing everything in the dishwasher.

"I'll see you tonight."

Zion said. "Tonight. Be careful."

"Always."

Zion got dressed and then went to the garage to get his bike. He placed his Airpods in his ears and hit play on his Iphone. He slowly peddled out to the street. He needed to clear his head. Bob Marley came pumping through the earphones.

He peddled hard and fast. He was at top speed when he came to the end of his route. He flew pass the stop sign. He suddenly slammed on the brakes leaving a long black tire mark behind him. He climbed off the bike and took a seat at a near by bench.

He took a deep breath and then closed his eyes. He needed to enter his place of peace. Meditation was just one of the methods he used to center himself. He hoped on his bike and took a slow cruise back home.

After a much-needed shower he got dressed, grabbed his business material then headed out the door. Tupac pumped from the speakers as he drove. He pulled into the parking lot and noticed all the vehicles of his small team. Every other week they gather for a brainstorming session.

"How's everyone's morning going thus far?" He asked.

He took a seat at the head of the table. He pulled his Ipad from his sling bag. The group was ready to get things moving they're all go-getters. Zion was picky with his selection of people to join his team. The hour flew by. He didn't want to head home. All he would do is think about her.

He ordered a slice of banana bread and a white chocolate mocha frappuccino. He took a seat on the patio. He pulled his phone from his bag; there were no missed calls. He dialed Derek's number.

"Hey cuz. Its been a minute."

"It has. I've a ton on my mind." Zion said.

"I bet. Did you see what happened to Shake?"

Zion said. "That was him on the news."

"It was." Derek said.

A lost life is nothing to take lightly, but Zion was smiling just a little on the inside. He wanted to ask if Derek had seen Journey, but he didn't. He finished his meal before making his way to his ride.

"I'm going to call you once I get home."

"I'm on my way to the park to shoot around you're welcome to join me."

"I just might." Zion ended the call. He pulled the car into traffic and the smashed on the gas. He made a stop at the house before heading to the park.

"Hey cuz. What's up? No bike?"

Zion said. "I went out earlier.

Derek passed him the ball. He took a shot. He missed. Zion rebounded his own shot. He passed the ball to Derek.

"You up for a game of twenty one?" Derek asked.

"Let me warm up. You trying to get a win against a cold arm."

Derek laughed. "You act like you're an old man. You don't need time to warm up. You should be ready to play whenever you step onto the court."

"Said the guy who's been out her for an hour."

Derek took a shot, but missed it. He missed it on purpose. He hadn't beat Zion one on one in a long time. Derek was the one going to school to play ball. But for some reason Zion was a much better player.

"Hey guys."

Zion and Derek turned their attention to the voice. They both were happy to see her. Journey smiled. Zion stood still, he couldn't move. He couldn't take his eyes off of her. Derek bounced the ball a few times before passing it to her.

"How are you guys doing?" She asked.

"I'm good." Derek told her.

Zion said. "Better now."

She passed the ball back to Derek. He took a quick shot, made it. "Nice pass." He said. Journey strolled toward Zion. He wanted to run to her. But his feet wouldn't move.

She put her arms around him. He pulled her closer. He held her tight. She loved his embrace.

She whispered. "I'm sorry I didn't call."

"You're here now." He said.

Beverly pulled into the lot. She parked next to a beat up van. She slowly exited her sedan. She pulled her briefcase slash purse from the backseat. She checked her identification. Everything was in order.

She entered the building. The place was in need of a deep clean. The floors were dingy and the room smelled of sweat and cigarettes. She laid her ID on the counter.

"I'm here to see my client." She said.

"I need you to sign in."

She followed a large man back to a small room. The room was filled with a table and two wooden chairs. She placed her bag on the table. She never puts her purse on the floor. She's superstitious.

"He'll be here shortly. Do you need anything?" The mountain of a man asked. She smiled. She cleared her throat before answering.

"I'm all set here."

The man stood by the door. Frankie was lead in wearing his prison attire. He was much bigger than she remembered. His locks were shoulder length. But the lifeless mask still covered his face. He took the other chair. The guard chained him to the table.

Frankie smiled. He couldn't believe that she was sitting across from him. He wanted to wrap his hands around her thin long neck.

"How's life?" She asked.

"It goes on, no matter if I'm here or on the outside. The world keeps turning."

"Yes, you're right."

"Why are you here? And more importantly why am I here? We don't have any business. Or do we?"

"More than you know."

"Do tell."

She moved her purse. She leaned in. He did the same. They made eye contact. His breath was foul. She could barley stand the smell. She leaned back.

She said. "You know you're going to die in here."

"Life without the chance of parole. I know the meaning. But I'm living my best life."

He didn't connect the dots. He was high on power. He believed that he couldn't be touch. But was he wrong?

"I know you placed the hit on my son."

"Your son is bad for my business."

She told him. "You made a mistake that's bad for your health."

"I'm going back to my cell."

She stood, grabbed her bag. She slowly made her way to the door. "Enjoy your time here." She told him.

She exited the room. He called for the guard. But instead four inmates with ice picks entered the room. Frankie got it now. He was going to die in here.

Beverly climbed into her car. She turned on the radio. She pulled her cell from her bag.

"Hey babe, I'll be a little late. You need me to pick up anything from the store?"

She backed out, and then headed home.

# THE END

Thank you all for your support. Happy reading and God bless.
You can reach me at:

Facebook: Anthony L Wallace
Instagram: AnthonyWallace2706
Twitter: Anthonylwallace

Website: Anthonylwallace.lifevantage.com
Check my other books:
The color of love
The escort
Corner boy
Ellen
Bad Company

Milton Keynes UK
Ingram Content Group UK Ltd.
UKHW010217030124
435363UK00005B/495